UNORTHODOX SUCCESS SECRET SHAME

How I Stopped Feeling Like the World's Biggest Fake and Found Peace in Being Me

CHRIS FROLIC

ISBN 978-1-9992083-2-5

Chris Frolic Group Inc.
Toronto, Canada
www.chrisfrolic.com

Edited by Robin Frolic
Book Design and Typesetting by Najdan Mancic.

Also by Chris Frolic:
Requiem for My Rave: The Story of Anabolic Frolic,
Happy Hardcore, and Hullabaloo!
Available for sale today on Amazon.

Contributing Author:
The Business of Stage Hypnosis, The Best of the Stage Hypnosis Center
The Ronning Guide to Modern Stage Hypnosis

I dedicate this book to Geoff Ronning.

CONTENTS

HOW TO USE THIS BOOK

This book is a collection of thoughts about my history and experience dealing with debilitating imposter syndrome. Completing this book is part of my journey. In a lot of ways I feel like I've come out the other side of this, so I wanted to create the book that I wished someone had given me years ago, when I was in the depths of my crisis.

I would have felt less alone.
I would have felt seen.
I would have had hope for a solution.

Back in my crisis, I desperately wished I had someone to model after, to make my life easier. If that's a role I can play for you now, that would make me happy.

Back then, I didn't even know what imposter syndrome was. I was suffering alone.

Like everything I do, I didn't follow the rules when creating this book. I was inspired by my desire to help people like me, so I created what made sense to me.

This book is written in the style I best communicate: I tell my own story. I used to think that my story didn't have value because I was too different, my story was too wild, and there was nothing to learn from me unless you were me. I've now learned how wrong I was. That's part of getting over my feelings of being a fake. There is value—a lot of value!—in telling my story. The fact that it is so unique is what makes what I have to say so valuable.

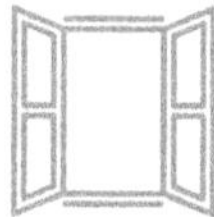

Every chapter ends with a powerful Action Step or Steps, contained in a separate box. To get the most out of this experience, I invite you to really take time with it and see how it applies to your own life. Don't move on until you have a response to each question. Write out the answer in your own journal. As you move through the book your answers will evolve. This is normal. Give yourself the space you need to impact your life from this experience.

So, who am I to write this book? Let's start with my accomplishments. I'm the co-founder of StealthSeminar.com, the leader in the automated webinar business. It launched in 2010, made a profit from day one, has created over a billion dollars for its users, and today it is bigger than it has ever been. In the 1990s I was a hugely successful DJ known as Anabolic Frolic, with the best-selling electronic music series of that decade, "Happy2bHardcore". I was an architect of the original rave movement as a promoter of one of the most revered and celebrated rave promotions, "Hullabaloo!" I was the host of the highest-rated online dance music show of 2000, Happy Hour. I have a published memoir about that part of my life called Requiem for My Rave. Following my DJ career, I spent five years as a comedy stage hypnotist, appearing on television and doing shows across Canada, where I live.

Now here's the thing: I accomplished all of the above while never having graduated high school. That was a secret shame of mine for most of my life. I clearly have a solid history of "making shit happen", and yet because of my unconventional background, the things I did, and how different they all were, I didn't see it that way. Despite how successful my efforts were, I felt like the biggest fraud in the world.

I didn't start out feeling that way. It got worse over time. The more money I made, the worse I felt.

I stand before you today firmly on the other side of this story. Nowadays, I like to help people like me—those with unconventional backgrounds who have achieved incredible success, yet still feel like fakes that have fooled the world and are too ashamed to admit that this is their problem.

This is what this book is about.

I'm able to speak it, and share what changed, and how I changed. My hope is that my book might find and speak to the people that really need to hear this. I look forward to what new thinking it will create in your own mind and what new possibilities it might open.

Something in you chose to read this book, and that tells me you're ready to change your situation. It all starts there, so you've already done the hardest part.

I believe in you.

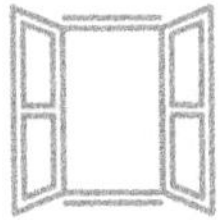

> *What is your intention from reading this book?*

PART ONE

THE CRISIS

CHAPTER ONE

I'M GOING TO DIE

"I think I'm having a heart attack," I told Robin, my wife. It was the only explanation I had for the pain in my chest. I felt pressure, like a contraction, all around the center of my chest. It was like someone was pushing their fist into my ribcage. I didn't know what to do. I was terrified that I was going to die.

After asking a few questions about other symptoms, Robin said, "It's not a heart attack. It's anxiety. You spent so many years worried about money, now that it isn't a worry, your mind has to find something else to worry about."

Robin tracked down my bottle of Ativan, prescribed to me years earlier to help with flying to Australia. I took one, hoping Robin was right.

I had no other choice but to trust Robin in that moment. In my mind, I figured if I collapsed on the floor, Robin could call 911. I would wait until that moment before going to the hospital. I guess enough of me suspected I wasn't actually dying, and I wanted to avoid the shame of showing up in the emergency room as a hypochondriac.

The tranquilizers began to work. The fear was subsiding. Whatever it was I was feeling in my chest wasn't an actual heart attack, because it wasn't getting worse, it was getting better.

I wish I could say things got better from that day, but they didn't. I wish I could say I didn't fear having a heart attack again, but I did, regularly. I wish I could say I learned to get through these panic attacks without resorting to tranquilizers, but I didn't, not for a long while.

Why was I feeling this way? I had so much to celebrate and be grateful for. Robin was correct in saying I used to worry about money for years, and now I didn't need to anymore. After living precariously my entire adult life, I had finally "made it" financially. My latest venture, a webinar tech business, was a financial success. I still have an ATM receipt from that time from the bank with my checking account showing a balance of $723,881.82. It was cash money just sitting there. Every month I received more money than I knew how to spend. I achieved all the things I wanted in life. I had wanted a home for my family, where my kids would have their own bedrooms. We then found our dream home, in our dream neighborhood.

I was so worried about my ability to keep generating this kind of money in the future, I paid the house off within three years rather than carry a mortgage.

I had literally made millions of dollars, in real money in my hands, not pretend paper money, or stock valuations, or crypto fortunes. Yet I was terrified it could all disappear overnight.

The problem was that I felt like a fraud.

How I got here made no sense. I must have fooled everyone. I was making millions of dollars in tech, and I'm a high school dropout. No one taught me to do what I do. I had to figure it out on my own.

I kept rerunning my history in my head. Before the tech biz, I was a comedy stage hypnotist. Yes, that's as much of a non-sequitur as it reads. Before that, I was one of the best-selling DJs in the world and one of the most beloved rave promoters of the 1990s. Huh? Before that, I had worked at a video game store since I was twelve years old. When I was eighteen I moved to work at their head office, traveling the country while setting up new franchises and training the new owners on how to run their business. Where is the string that ties this all together?

It was such an absurd story. It felt like these things all sort of just… happened. It had to have been sheer luck more than anything else. "Right place, right time," was my belief.

With my previous ventures I had had various degrees of success, but the financial component evaded me until my most recent company.

It was the huge inflow of cash, combined with my unorthodox story of getting here, that really made me feel like a fraud. I fooled everyone; there was no other explanation.

And that left me feeling so unhappy. I felt like I was in over my head, and I had no idea how to transition out.

I felt so guilty. Guilty about how I felt, and why I felt it, and how it was affecting the people around me.

I felt so scared. Scared that everything would go up in smoke, and I'd have no ability to do anything after this. My only thought about how to create income was to rent out the basement of my house as an apartment. I didn't see any potential in myself for doing anything else.

I was scared I was going to die, either by dropping dead of a heart attack or going to sleep and never waking up again. What would happen to my family without me to support them?

And I felt so ashamed that these were my problems. Who am I to complain about anything? I literally have everything I wanted, including a happy marriage and amazing children.

I couldn't speak of my negative feelings, because my shame was too great.

That was me at my worst. I was in this state for six long years. The money rolled in and I dealt with fear, guilt, and shame. I spent every moment feeling like a fraud.

I estranged myself from mostly everyone. I withdrew. I did my best to avoid talking to my business partner, Geoff. It was ridiculous, but I couldn't control it. I didn't even know what I was doing. I was driven by primal fear.

Finally, in my crisis, I hit my lowest point. I had to pull myself out before I destroyed everything.

What in my story do you relate with?

CHAPTER TWO

I WAS KING OF THE IMPOSTERS

I suffered for years for an unknown reason. Despite my outward success, the money I made, the things I owned, I was extremely unhappy and miserable. Then I came across the term "Imposter Syndrome" and things started to make more sense for me.

Wikipedia.com describes imposter syndrome as: *Impostor syndrome (also known as impostor phenomenon, impostorism, fraud syndrome or the impostor experience) is a psychological pattern in which an individual doubts their skills, talents, or accomplishments and has a persistent internalized fear of being exposed as a "fraud". Despite external evidence of their competence, those experiencing this phenomenon remain convinced that they are frauds and do not deserve all they have achieved. Individuals with impostorism incorrectly attribute their success to luck, or interpret it as a result of deceiving others into thinking they are more intelligent than they perceive themselves to be.*

I was living my life feeling like an imposter. My case was even more severe because I was living as an actual imposter—I had created an alias for the webinar company I had co-founded. I had decided early on that it wouldn't serve my tech business if it was revealed that a former DJ and rave promoter had hand-coded all of our software, with no outside help or assistance. Why would anyone trust the work of a hypnotist and high-school dropout?

Looking back, my achievement is amazing, but in my mind it felt like I had fooled everyone. Nobody could know this secret.

So I created a fake name, as generic as I could make it: Greg Fisher. That person was the brains behind the software. I let my partner be the public face, and I toiled away in the background with no credit other than my monthly dividends.

Even my own staff only interacted with me as "Greg Fisher".

It wasn't meant to be a big thing, because at the start we didn't even know if this project would work. But as the business kept growing, my identity became a bigger and bigger secret.

The worst part was that I could not feel the success of the business, since I continued to think I fooled everyone. Millions of users were successfully using the software I created by myself with, as I phrased it, "duct tape and Popsicle sticks". They were getting value from it, because it worked. It was the product of my creativity and ingenuity. Yet I was scared all the time I would be outed as not knowing what I was doing, and it could all go poof.

I made a ton of money and every month I was worried that could be the last check I would ever see. I feared I'd never do anything as big as this.

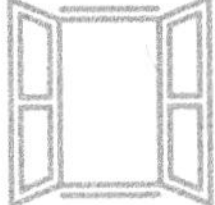

When was the last time you found yourself feeling like an imposter?

CHAPTER THREE

I SUFFERED FOR YEARS

One of my biggest regrets is how many years I suffered needlessly because I didn't value my own work.

Here are some pics from over twenty years ago, during February 1999. This is me DJing in front a sea of people at the International Center, just outside of Toronto. People paid and traveled to come to see me. I had sold hundreds of thousands of CDs by this time, and my rave company, Hullabaloo!, was at its peak.

When this event was over, I went home to my one-bedroom basement apartment. I had abandoned my piece-of-crap car in the street about a month before these pics were taken, because I had no money to pay for insurance or fix the car.

I lived without a car for fourteen years after this.

I want to make this even more clear: I had just had 5,000 people buy tickets to see me, and I was broke! If I calculated the hourly wage of the months of planning and risk that went into putting an event on of this size, not to mention my value as an attraction—I was working for below minimum wage. I lived in apartments, often scraping by, until 2012.

I didn't value the experience I was creating for all of my patrons. I was fixated on keeping prices low and only making a small bit of profit, in some misguided attempt at not looking greedy, combined with working-class guilt.

And I suffered greatly because of it. The sad thing was, I was still accused of "being in it for the money". People would do bar-napkin math and guess that I was making 100x more what the reality was. So, my suffering wasn't even quieting those critics. I did it for nothing!

My real fans, the ones that truly valued this unique experience I was creating, I'm sure would have told me the event was priceless.

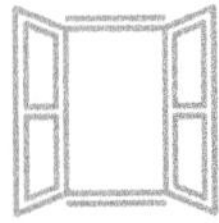

When in the last 6 months have you found yourself suffering unnecessarily from being unable to value yourself properly?

To see video from this exact rave, if you are curious what it was all about:

WWW.CHRISFROLIC.COM/BONUS/

CHAPTER FOUR

IMPOSTER SYNDROME IS A PRESENTING SYMPTOM

In medical terms, a "presenting symptom" is the reason someone seeks help with a medical problem. A cough that lasts for weeks is a common presenting symptom for tuberculosis, for example; the patient doesn't yet know they have tuberculosis, but they know this cough needs to get checked out.

Just as the cough is not the tuberculosis itself, imposter syndrome is a symptom and not the underlying issue.

I didn't realize this at first. I thought imposter syndrome *was* my problem. I believed I needed to treat *that*.

The anxiety I was feeling, the fear, and the guilt: they were all tied together. All were presenting symptoms of a much deeper problem.

A lack of *sense of self.*

I didn't believe in myself. I didn't know who I was. I thought I did: I'm a father, husband, and entrepreneur. Those are all pretty clear, so what else is there? Yet the feelings continued.

The first step is to recognize the difference between the presenting symptom and the actual thing.

Where in your own life do you feel like an imposter?

What changes for you if you consider that the imposter syndrome is a presenting symptom and not the actual problem?

I BOUGHT MY WAY OUT OF AN EXISTENTIAL CRISIS (OR SO I THOUGHT)

n 2012 my life was on a trajectory I hadn't experienced before, with real financial stability. I had huge monthly dividends arriving and had moved out of my apartment into a rented house. I had a bank account flush with cash, and for the first time in my life nothing to worry about.

There was one fly in the ointment though—my brain was so conditioned to worry, to my precarious life, to living on the edge. When I solved a huge part of that, it needed to find something else to latch on to. It settled on my health.

Suddenly I had massive health anxiety. Every time I got winded, I thought I was going to have a heart attack. Every time I felt my heart beating, it felt abnormal. The anxiety trap I found myself in often triggered a racing heart, which made me even more scared.

Then my mind went to cancer. A benign lump on my body that I've had for 10 years, that had been checked out and cleared through MRI a number of times, all of a sudden had new menace. I was convinced something had changed. It had grown, and this time it was going to kill me.

This constant health anxiety triggered an even worse outcome: a full-blown existential crisis. For about five months, through-out the entire summer of 2012, I was consumed with thoughts of death, and of what happens (or doesn't happen) afterward. From the moment I woke up, to the moment I fell asleep, that awareness of my death was haunting me. It was unrelenting, exhausting, and brutal.

All of this was because my life was at its best.

I can recall watching the opening ceremonies of the 2012 London Olympics that summer. There was a part of it telling the story of the industrial revolution, about how man conquered nature, with the sounds of trees falling. It had some of the most beautiful music I can remember hearing, and I bawled my eyes out.

I was a wreck and I had no idea what to do.

Finally, towards the end of that summer, a memory came back to me. It was of my youth and the countless hours I spent in arcades. I thought about my young wish of having a pinball machine in my home. What a luxury!

And I realized in that moment, with my income and my home, I could actually do it.

I found a pinball community online. I researched and found an amazing pinball machine, a brand new state-of-the-art one. "New in box", as we say in the pinball community. It was a lot of money but Robin told me, "You deserve it." With Robin's blessing, I ordered it.

I felt like a kid at Christmas. These were feelings I hadn't felt in a very long time: the anticipation, the excitement. Those feelings of being a kid again overtook the existential crisis and health anxiety. I was so happy.

The game arrived in a huge box. We unpacked it, set it up in the basement, and it was awesome.

It was so awesome, I bought another pinball a month later. And then another. And then another. And then I filled all available space in the basement with five pinball machines. Robin enjoyed decorating the basement to look like an arcade.

We had people over. I joined the local pinball league and made the first new friends I had made in over a decade. It was glorious.

And when it came time to buy a new home, we made sure it could support my crazy idea of building a secret arcade. We disqualified homes that could not do that. Then we found our perfect home. I filled it with fifteen pinball machines and a Pac Man machine and custom neon and tokens and branded merchandise featuring my arcade's name, Frolic's Arcade. I fully realized this wild idea I had.

But the joy didn't last. I had only put a Band-aid on a gunshot wound.

I hadn't dealt with the real work that I needed to address my underlying crisis.

I was still so vulnerable. When internet trolls attacked me and my arcade out of envious resentment, they weren't just criticizing some things I owned, they were inflicting terrible damage on a hurting human being.

I was still struggling with brutal imposter syndrome and anxiety, and my personal relationships were being affected. Buying things was no longer helping me.

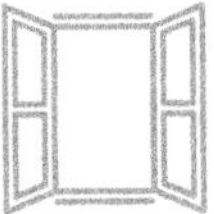

Where have you been applying Band-aids to yourself in your own life?

CHAPTER SIX

THE SADDEST MAN I EVER SAW

Many years ago when I was still DJing, I was waiting to be picked up at the Arrivals section of Chicago O'Hare Airport. I was standing by the driveway where cars picked up waiting passengers. Beside me were a teenage girl and her mother. They had a few suitcases, returning from who-knows-where together.

As I waited for my pickup, a car pulled up in front of the mom and daughter. A man got out. Slumped. Silent. He just seemed… so sad.

The scene got even sadder. This man went to the trunk and opened it. The mom and daughter put their luggage in and got in the car. The sad man got in the driver's seat, and… drove away.

There was no interaction between the man and the mom and daughter. This was twenty years ago, so this was not an Uber or private car pickup.

With horror I realized I had just witnessed a terribly dysfunctional family. There was no greeting between them, no love. The daughter did not acknowledge the father, following the lead of the mom.

I'll never know what was truly going on with that family, but it was so sad that the sight of it scarred me for life. I've recounted this story many times, both to my own family and others. I swore I'd never be that man. I'd never let the chain of events happen that resulted in that scene I saw that day.

Whatever happened to them started a long time earlier. I would prioritize my family, and never let that happen. I would take corrective action, and have, when caught in my own pits of unhappiness.

When I've found myself at crossroads, to take corrective action or do nothing, I've taken the action. To do nothing would over time make me into a version of the sad man I saw that day, defeated and broken.

Last September I was returning from four days away and Robin picked me up at the nearest subway station, to give me a lift back to our house. Our two kids were in the back seat.

"Hi Daddy!" I was cheerfully welcomed as I got into the car.

I thanked my kids for coming for the trip to pick me up. They could have easily stayed at home while Robin did the ten-minute round trip.

"I remember you telling me about that dad at the airport," said my younger child. He was doing his part in not recreating that scene for me. Having a strong family bond takes effort and my kids have followed my lead. My kids could have stayed home, but they took action, and came for the trip because they knew it would be better to greet me in a nice way when I had been gone.

Some of my greatest lessons come from my own mistakes, but if I can learn from someone else's, I'd rather learn that way.

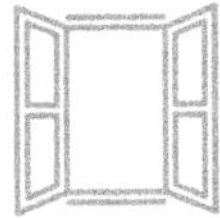

Imagine you were me that day, standing at the airport arrivals curb and witnessed the sight of this family encounter. What lesson could you apply to yourself to ensure this doesn't happen to you?

CHAPTER SEVEN

WHEN YOU'RE AN IMPOSTER, THE BIGGEST FAKE YOU ARE IS TO YOURSELF

The greatest crime of feeling as I did, as suffering as I did, for years, was that I didn't see my own success in front of my eyes. I was the one that accomplished these things. Whether it was through sales, tickets, profit, users, or other people's successes using my products, there were many measures of my value.

Now I understand this one hard truth: The world didn't see me as a fake. They saw my value. I was only a fake through my own eyes.

In a sense, I was fooling only one person: myself.

Who do you think you're fooling?

Imagine you achieved this clarity that you were the one fooling yourself. What would change for you?

PART TWO
THE
AWAKENING

THE DAY MY LIFE CHANGED

It is so easy for me to dazzle people with the "greatest hits" version of my story. I can easily talk about the things I've done, to show the pictures and video. I've done some cool stuff, no question.

I find other people often perceive me as the most interesting person in the room, and for a long time it was fun to be that for people. I enjoyed getting to tell my stories. The problem was, I was only telling one slice of it.

No one ever heard of the struggle, unless formed into some sort of "humble brag" story. They never heard the actual truth. I didn't know how to share those grimmer aspects, and frankly, I was ashamed to speak of them.

My learned strategy of compartmentalizing my stress, anxiety, and trauma allowed me to accomplish great things. I could project my strengths and hide my weaknesses. It was "fake it 'til you make it", but then keep faking it, never stop faking it. Always I had to fake that I had all my shit together.

It worked, until it became untenable. My relationship with my business partner was difficult because I was afraid to talk to him. I avoided him because I was good at avoiding my problems. I had become, in fact, a master at avoiding my problems.

The reason I was avoiding my partner was simply because he got angry on a phone call with me.

Our service had had an outage. I had been feeling over my head for a long time, not knowing what to do about it, and on this day as he was upset, I totally owned all of that failure.

My experience of that phone call was that my secret as a fraud was totally exposed. My best wasn't good enough anymore. I didn't know what I was doing, and I was letting my partner down.

I didn't understand why at the time, but I was so terrified of being yelled at again, everything in me avoided being in that situation. I hardly spoke with him from that point forward. We'd go half a year without speaking, while we ran a multi-million-dollar business together.

I knew what I was doing was not rational, but it didn't matter. The survival instinct in me was so strong, I couldn't resist it. This period of life had me making the most money I had ever made and at the same time I was the most miserable. My unhappiness was present every single day. It went on like this for years.

(And here's an interesting note: my partner, Geoff, was an advance reader of this book. I was curious to ask him now about his experience of that phone call. I knew my experience and his could be vastly different. It still affected me how it affected me, but I was genuinely interested now to revisit it and hear his version. Would he agree with my description of anger and yelling or was that simply the lens I saw it through? I am finally in a place strong enough to ask. Geoff revealed he had no memory of that call. What I experienced as a house of cards collapsing was only from my end.)

Finally, I had had enough. I asked my wife to find me a therapist, since Robin was periodically in therapy and knew about these things.

"I can't do that for you, you have to find someone yourself. This is a personal decision that you have to make," Robin said.

I understand why Robin did this. You have to be the person to pull yourself out. No one can do it for you. (Robin has since added, "If someone isn't ready to find themselves a therapist, they're not ready for the work of therapy.")

I think it took me another year to finally start poking around websites of psychotherapists, looking at bios. I found someone local to me that I could drive to.

I arranged my first visit. I vividly recall barely making it there. I was so overwhelmed with anxiety. Everything in me was telling me not go. It was a war just to make myself go in.

It didn't get any better once I began. As I started talking about why I was there, my whole body was overrun with a desire to go to sleep. My brain was trying to protect me. "Go to sleep," it said.

Fortunately, I was in the office of a professional. They told me nothing bad was going to happen to me there. I was in a safe space. They'd make sure I'm fine. They covered me with a blanket. I had no choice but to trust them and I made it through that first session.

Over the next few sessions, I began to learn where these behaviors were coming from: I learned them as a child, in the face of my screaming father. A child can only cower and make themselves small, and I learned how to do that throughout my childhood. Those learned behaviors stayed with me as an adult, and only got worse and worse without being corrected.

It was to the point where I had subconsciously treated my business partner as my father. I felt like I had to hide from him.

When I had the realization of how things from our childhood affect us for the rest of our life, something changed in me. I finally had some clarity and understanding for what was happening. Once I started to understand it, I could break the habit from recurring.

I continue to go to therapy twice a week. The conversations have evolved from the really obvious surface-level anxiety to a much more deeper understanding of how I operate and the person I am.

I now enjoy telling my story, the whole story, with no shame. I see part of my role now in the world is to share this whole story, for whoever can benefit from that.

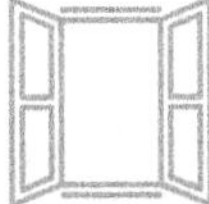

Imagine you had the ability to powerfully tell your own unique and valuable story. Who benefits from that?

CHAPTER NINE

BEING AUTHENTIC

During my time in therapy I was introduced to the concept of being "authentic". As soon as I heard it, it really struck me.

I realized immediately I have been a master of "Fake It 'Til You Make It". It did work for me, quite successfully, many times in my life.

I can't even speak against that as a strategy. It certainly can be effective when you are starting out.

But I'm in a different place today. I'm over faking it. Now I strive to be 100% authentic with everyone I deal with in my life.

I speak openly about all of my challenges. This is far different than before, when I believed it's easier just to promote the positive and hide the negatives, or somehow that by sharing the negatives, that might prevent me from reaching the success I was after.

The feedback I've received is that people really appreciate when they hear me share my challenges—whatever they are—because they are often facing similar things.

I still wrestle with self-doubt, anxiety, fear of failure (or success), and planning for all the negative "what ifs".

But now I share them. I throw them out into the world. I find this takes their power away. It makes me feel better and it seems to help others by hearing it.

People far more successful than I am wrestle with this. People that have more money than me worry about losing it all. People in glass tower offices fear they'll be found out as fakes. We all feel like we don't know what the hell we are doing.

I felt better about myself when I learned that other people have the same challenges.

How has reading about my struggles affected you?

Who would you become if you affected other people in this same way?

CHAPTER TEN

NO, YOU DIDN'T FOOL THE WORLD. YOU CAN'T FEEL LIKE A FAKE UNLESS YOU'VE DONE SOMETHING

"Whoa… I stopped hearing anything you said after that first sentence," said my friend.

I was sharing the outline of an article I was writing, about my devastating imposter syndrome and how I learned to get over it and love myself.

"Which one? That you can't feel like a fake unless you've done something?"

"Yes. Holy crap, my life just shifted. You know those moments of insight when they describe that shift? It is literally a whole different and affirming way to look at my life. That sentence is a shift on a cellular level for me."

I was taken aback by her reaction. And then I remembered a common truth: the things we find easiest, we don't value. I was doing it right here. I was sharing my "cocktail napkin" notes… something I had written out in a minute or two shortly before our call and wanted to share with someone. I had thought nothing of it, other than that it was an idea for an article.

I've learned enough to recognize this habit, so I was able to stop my dismissal of my thoughts and circle back to the fact that I had come up with something valuable.

"Thank you for sharing your reaction with me. It was really valuable to reflect what I had," I replied.

My thinking behind that statement has come from the fact that only in very recent years have I begun to appreciate everything I have done and accomplished.

It has become so crystal clear for me: *you can't feel like a fake unless you have had some kind of success or achievement.* In a sense, the imposter feelings are *evidence* of the scope of your achievement. The bigger an imposter you feel like, the bigger your achievement.

I faked my foot through the door multiple times in my life, but once I was through that door, it was all on me. No amount of faking can create actual results. Only you delivering creates results.

I couldn't fake my way to my DJ series selling ten times what the record label had projected.

I couldn't fake my way to selling out events with everyone paying to come see me.

I might have gotten myself on TV to do a demo of stage hypnosis with no experience, but when I showed up I did an amazing bit on live TV, one so impressive that I used it for the rest of my career and it got me immediate bookings.

I thought I fooled the world by creating software with no training or education, but I couldn't fake that millions of people used it and got tremendous value from it.

I was caught up in my own head thinking that I was a fake, when the evidence was always there of my success. I now see it and appreciate it for what it is.

People who do nothing and achieve nothing will never feel like a fake. Only those that actually have done something feel that way. In my case, the crushing imposter syndrome I lived with for years was fed by the scope of my success. I did some awesome things. I can now appreciate them and know I did that.

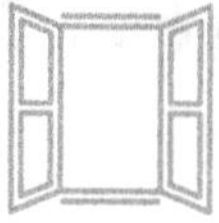

Think of a victory in your life that you feel you faked your way through.

Now, hear my words: You can't feel like a fake unless you've done something.

Imagine a moment in the future when you realize that statement is true. How does it impact you to realize that those feelings of having been a fake are the literal evidence of the size of your success?

CHAPTER ELEVEN

WHAT IS REAL WORK?

was recently watching The Chef Show on Netflix. It's hosted by Jon Favreau (movie director of Iron Man, Lion King, and The Jungle Book, as well as being an actor). He was visiting Wolfgang Puck's steakhouse in Las Vegas and was grilling steaks in front of Wolfgang. He then handed one of them to Wolfgang to inspect. Wolfgang cut it open, saw the perfect medium rare, and they had this exchange:

Wolfgang: *Jon, you know what? Forget about the movie business. You can come and work with us and get a real job. Your father would be proud of you. Like, "Finally!"*

Jon: *Yes. "Finally." It's true. Doing something.*

Wolfgang: *Yeah, doing something real.*

I lost my breath from this exchange. They were being facetious, but were talking about a commonly held idea. Here's

Jon Favreau, director of multiple billion-dollar movies, being teased about how his father isn't proud of his work.

This cut me down because I've lived it.

My father worked in construction and on farms his whole life. In his seventies now, he still grows vegetables on his land. He only knows hard work.

He has never understood what I did, or what I do, or how it's possible that I've had success doing it.

His lack of understanding is so great that he skipped me over in his will, making sure my children (his grandchildren) get their share of his estate and I don't, by handing the responsibility for my children's shares to my sibling.

When I confronted him about his decision (and the insult to put my children's inheritance in the hands of someone else for safekeeping) he flat-out told me he doesn't get what I do, so what's to stop me from wasting his money?

"Christopher, you don't have a job. You don't work anywhere."

He has no comprehension of the things I do, or that you can leverage your mind and creativity. That you can create value and not just trade your physical labor for money.

These Hollywood people joking about it on the show made me feel seen. I also realized that this experience must be so common, to have them talking about it like they did. I wasn't alone.

I'm sure these insidious lessons I absorbed from childhood fed my later imposter syndrome and are a big part of why it took me a long time to value my work.

I can hear my father's voice in my head: *How DARE you make the kind of money you make without going into a job every day?*

Seeing this exchange on the show made me feel better about my own experience with my father. It's a generational thing. Then I affirmed to myself that I wouldn't fall into the same trap with my own kids. If they end up doing things I just don't understand and go about it in ways I don't get, that will be okay.

I pride myself on doing things for the first time. I will no longer be angry at my father for not seeing it.

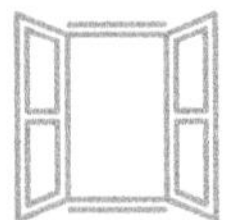

Who are the people in your life that have in-fluenced your self-worth, perhaps in a way you didn't even realize?

Imagine that with this clarity, their power over you fell away to nothing. Why would that be important to you?

CHAPTER TWELVE

THE DIFFICULTY IN CLAIMING YOUR VALUE

I got my first job by offering to work for free. At age twelve I walked into a newly opened computer and video game store and somehow had the courage to ask for a job. When I was turned down, working for free was my solution. They accepted.

I worked for free for the next several months, then below minimum wage (because I wasn't even at legal working age). I was paid $3.00 an hour, when minimum wage was $3.90 at the time. I was just so happy to make any money.

When I was eighteen, I was invited by the owner of that same company to leave home and move to Toronto while he started to franchise the business. "I can't afford to pay you anything right now," he said. "You'll live with me in Toronto." Once again, I was working for free.

I eventually started getting paid again, although I was making essentially minimum wage for highly skilled and valuable work, as I was flying around the country opening new franchises and training their owners.

And then a few years later the company ran into trouble. The owner once again asked me to work for free. This time he proposed *I collect unemployment insurance while I still went in to work.*

I accepted.

My work was never valued. I never developed the ability to value my own work, between my lessons from this company and my own father who worked his ass off his whole life, broke his body, and never made much money.

When I became a DJ, I did not know how to value myself. I took whatever I was offered. A lot of my bookings were me accepting the gig, and then being handed some money after, which I didn't contest or debate. I felt lucky to get anything.

When I was a rave promoter, I was sleeping on the floor of my office, unable to pay for a real place to live, because I didn't know how to value myself. Later, at the peak of my success, I was selling out events of 5000. I was still living in a basement apartment because I was afraid of raising ticket prices by even

$5, which would have made a massive difference to my life. I was charging just barely enough to squeak by.

The biggest change in my life was when I co-founded my webinar company. The plan was that I would take care of all the tech, while my partner would handle all sales and customers. And he did one other very important job… he protected me from myself.

We split the profits 50/50, and he made sure there were plenty. For the first time in my life I was not living in a subsistence way. I had money in the bank for emergencies. Our cat needed surgery and I was able to pay for it. We moved out of our apartment into a rented house. We bought a car after not owning one for more than a decade. We purchased a home and quickly paid it off.

My money problems were solved, but that only happened because I had a partner making sure I got mine.

Now that I'm in this most recent part of my life, as I seek out what's next, I wanted to prove to myself I could do it alone. For the first time in my life, I'm claiming my value.

I've spent the last few years in therapy and self-work, and I finally understand who I am. And even more than that: not just who I am, but how *valuable* I am.

The first essential piece of this was to recover from my imposter syndrome. I had to see that all these things I've done and have been involved in didn't just happen. I made them happen. I needed to fully own that.

One doesn't get to where I am in life by luck. *No longer will I diminish my accomplishments by seeing them that way.*

And how does one put a price on understanding their own value?

Well, I did, because doing that was an important part of my recovery.

I am the sum total of all my life's experiences, lessons, and mistakes. There's only one of me in the entire universe. That's pretty awesome when you think about it.

Where that thinking led me was that everything I do now has a million dollar price attached. One day of my time is worth a million dollars, because I now have the ability to create that type of value. I can feel my own worth, and when I let others experience it, they can also feel it.

I no longer play the losing game of trying to guess what someone can afford. I have declared my value to myself and everyone else, and I inhabit that space. My goal, whether or not they can afford that price, is that they see it and they want it.

The impact I want to make in the world means leveraging those that have this ability to play at this level with me.

I'm writing this book as someone who charges a million dollars for their time. You're getting the best I have to give.

And that's where things have changed for me.

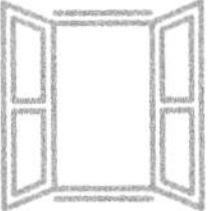

Just suppose you had clarity in this moment of what the next simple step would be toward claiming your own value. How would it change what you do tomorrow?

CHAPTER THIRTEEN

I HAD MORE IN COMMON WITH A HOMELESS MAN THAN I REALIZED

Some time ago a coach I knew shared a story about the year he spent volunteering in a homeless shelter. One day this homeless man came in, with absolutely no possessions except three plastic bags. He had been robbed at a park and all his meager possessions were stolen. His one remaining possession was an old cell phone. The robbers had grabbed it, but it dropped on the ground and the battery fell off. They took the battery but didn't bother with the battered old phone.

He wasn't looking to be coached to get off the streets. He didn't want to leave his way of life. But he did wonder if he could be coached to help with getting a new battery for his phone.

The coach helped him work out a strategy to go collect cans for recycling, the one way he knew how to make money. He knew which stores put their cans out when. He knew which parks had the best cans in the trash. Over three weeks he accumulated enough to get a replacement battery for his phone.

He came back for one last visit to the coach to show his now functioning phone. He was so happy, because now he could call his friends on the East Coast again. These were people he had known for decades that he stayed in contact with, even as he lived homeless in Los Angeles. He knew they would be worried about him during his time without a phone.

The homeless man went on to explain that he was homeless by choice. He didn't want to leave the streets. It was how he chose to live his life, unencumbered by society. The only contact he wanted was his old friends.

When I first heard this story, it was so alien to me that someone would choose that type of life. It was a nice story, but hard for me to understand.

A few years ago I was attending a four-day training in downtown Toronto. For four days I woke up early, showered, got dressed, and then got on the subway near my house to travel downtown to the hotel.

By the third day I could feel myself wanting to scream on the commute. The schedule was unbearable to me. Yet it was the same routine undertaken by millions of people in my city for their entire working lives.

I then remembered that homeless man and thought of my own history. I reflected on the years I lived on the edge, precarious, broke, bankrupt, but refusing to compromise how I wanted to live.

I realized I could not be paid enough money to do that commute every day. It was all I could do just to get through four days of it.

And in that moment I connected with the uncompromising freedom that that homeless man felt. I began to feel better about that part of my life. It was a choice I had made. A powerful choice. A choice for freedom above all else. I was no longer going to feel bad for myself for all the years I struggled. I had chosen it, because there was no other way I'd want to live.

Just like the homeless man, I was living aligned with my value of freedom over everything.

I now realize I had way more in common with that homeless man than I could appreciate at the time. I'm thankful to have heard that story, as it gave me peace later about my own life.

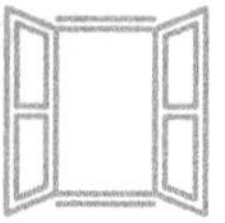

What part of your life might you have regret about, but when looked at through the lens of an uncompromising value, you realize there was no other way it could have gone?

CHAPTER FOURTEEN

MY UNCONVENTIONAL EDUCATION

've done a lot of stuff, and gone about them in my own unorthodox ways, and this certainly includes my education.

I never had any college or university education. I didn't even get a high school diploma. Yet now I look back at how much my education never stopped, no matter whether I was in school or not.

In high school I lost interest in being there. I'm not sure why exactly, but at some point I did the least possible to scrape by. I see now this had nothing to do with intelligence, and there was just something about the school experience that didn't work for me.

I never even made friends at high school, since I showed up a minute before the bell rang and was out of there seconds after the last bell. I had school acquaintances, but no one I developed a friendship with.

I did have something going on that was capturing me outside of school though, and that was my part-time job. That ended up being my social group, and I hung out with people much older than me. I had a ton of responsibility at a young age running that store, and when I joined the head office I took on a huge role with the company.

When my time there ended and I went on to pursue what was next, I saw my lack of a high school diploma as a huge liability. Finding work would be hard if I tried to succeed in the regular work force. I didn't know how to value the eight years of business apprenticeship I'd just had, both learning good skills and learning from the mistakes I observed. Yet those skills served me very well as I was able to apply them to my next chapter.

I continued to read and study things on my own as I developed interest in them.

I'm also grateful I found my path as an entrepreneur. Being an entrepreneur means you get to make up your own rules and apply those life lessons.

I bring this up because I want people to realize they are always learning, no matter what situation they are in. There are so many different ways to learn beyond being in a classroom. Life is a great teacher. Sometimes you can learn just by being around great people.

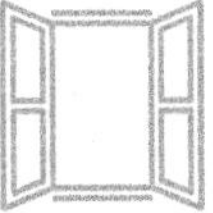

Just suppose you already know the answer for how you best learn. What is it? How can you do more of that?

CHAPTER FIFTEEN

JUST BECAUSE YOU WENT ABOUT IT ASS-BACKWARDS DOESN'T MEAN IT WASN'T EARNED

A big part of what fed my feelings of being a fraud and an imposter was that my story is so wild and different from anyone else's. Or at least anyone else I had come across.

I didn't follow the rules, usually because I didn't know there were any rules. I made it up. I solved whatever problem was in front of me and then moved on to the next one.

I realize now, as I write this, that is precisely what makes me valuable.

For many years I saw it another way. I felt I cheated my way through. I didn't earn it.

Instead of spending years at school, taking whatever courses I didn't care for, I simply learned enough about whatever subject I needed to solve the problem I was facing. And that's it. I was not an expert in that thing; I learned only enough to solve the problem.

If it was a programming challenge, instead of learning how to program from the ground up, I found a teaching tutorial online of how to do the small thing I wanted to do. I then modified it enough for my purposes. And then like Dr Frankenstein, I assembled one part into another and another, until I had a fully working "monster".

Instead of a celebratory shout of, "It's alive! It's alive!" at my accomplishment, I saw it as nothing, because I'd cobbled my solutions together.

I repeated this piecemeal learning when I started my pioneering online radio station in 2000, back before services existed to facilitate such things.

I repeated this when creating software for selling tickets for my events online, instead of using Ticketmaster.

I repeated this when I created an automated marketing system for my hypnosis business before tools like that existed.

I repeated this when creating my webinar company, a lot of which was repurposed technology from my radio streaming software.

All of this seemed unearned to me, because I hadn't made it all from scratch.

I now see it differently. I did do the hard work. I was freaking Dr Frankenstein and I created life where there was none. No one had ever done what I did before I did it. I had to learn enough to be able to follow tutorials and make different bits of code work together. I had to understand enough of several different programming languages to write the transitions that enabled these pieces to integrate into a greater whole. I had to be able to troubleshoot when things weren't clicking.

Because I operated outside the norms, I was never written up in magazines or attracted attention. That was mostly because I didn't see how what I did was special, and so I kept a low profile because of my shame.

But now I know I did earn it, and the fact that I did it ass-backwards is precisely why it was well-earned.

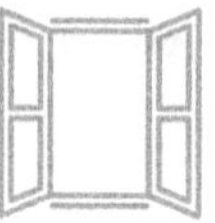

What "ass-backward" accomplishment do you have from your past, that perhaps you didn't value properly?

Imagine who you would be when you look back at it through this new lens?

CHAPTER SIXTEEN

IDENTITY VS ROLES WE PLAY

For a long time I did what most people do: I used external labels to describe myself. These were usually tied to what I did.

I was a DJ, a rave promoter, a hypnotist, and a tech co-founder.

Then for some years, I saw myself as a father, husband, and entrepreneur, in that order.

And then I learned that those things weren't my identity, but roles I inhabited. Roles are temporary. Some of them you can be in for a very long amount of time or an entire life, like a son or daughter, or a parent. But they are still just a role; one can decide to no longer be or consider themselves these roles.

People can get confused with their roles and identity. That is why someone who has their identity strongly linked with their work can have such a devastating time after retirement. When that role ends, their perceived identity also ends.

When this idea was first presented to me, I asked myself, "If I'm not a father, husband, and entrepreneur—if those are just roles I inhabit—then what am I?"

This was a very powerful question.

I really sat with it.

I remember lying in my bed that night, in that semi-awake state, and suddenly a word bubbled up out of my mental ether… "audacious".

And I remember thinking, "Huh. That's interesting. What does that mean for me?"

I looked up the definition online: *showing a willingness to take surprisingly bold risks.*

I started connecting the word audacious to all the major events of my life. I realized, "Holy crap, audacious actually fits all of them like a glove!"

During every major event in my life, during every major action I took, audaciousness was present. And I kept testing it, further and further back into my memories.

I even tied it to an event that happened when I was twelve years old. As I touched on earlier in this book, that year I walked into a computer and video game store and asked for a job.

That moment changed the trajectory of my life. Incredibly, everything that has happened in my life started with that audacious act when I was just twelve years old.

I even realize now that while I lost interest in school, and I've never had a piece of paper with my name on it because I've never graduated anything, I received an eight-year apprenticeship in business. It started when I was twelve years old until I left that company.

The skills I developed in business with them served me on my next adventure, as a rave promoter and DJ. This is the unconventional path I took.

I am audacious.

No matter how my life unfolds, that will always be true. It can't be taken away from me. Life events can't change and impact it. It just is.

I've had other words appear to me that I've added to my list, but it all started with that one and the clarity I got from experiencing it.

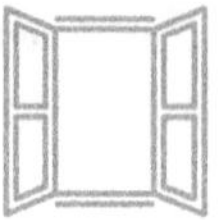

If you see yourself today through the lens of labels and roles you fill, what would change if you had another way to see yourself?

PART THREE

THE WAY FORWARD

CHAPTER SEVENTEEN

EVERYTHING CHANGED WITH THIS ONE REALIZATION

I vividly recall the moment everything changed. I had been working with my therapist for a while, telling her my stories.

"Chris, you've been carrying around the things that make you great as secret shame."

I've since distilled that into a simpler form:

The things that make me great, I carry as secret shame.

This was the game changer for me. All of my stories of how I cheated, how I was a fraud, how I faked my way through life, how I achieved the things I did the way I did them: I had such shame attached to those.

And yet, those exact things, and the ways I did them, are literally what makes me great.

My unique voice, my story: these are strengths.

Instead of trying to conform to a narrative I thought was how things were supposed to be done, and feeling bad about myself for the ways I didn't fit, it became the opposite. Now I see it in the past tense:

The things that make me great, I *carried* as secret shame.

But no more.

Now I'm proud of my story, how I went about it, and what I achieved in the face of everything.

I'm proud that I've done so many different things. I'm proud that I've reinvented myself. I'm all of these things.

It's from that place that I speak to you today.

What are the secret shames you carry, and how are they the exact things that make you great?

CHAPTER EIGHTEEN

ONE THING YOU CAN'T COPY FROM ME

During the years I felt like an imposter, I was under tremendous fear of my ideas being ripped off.

I would go through such lengths to hide and obfuscate my innovations. At the time I believed it was the only thing I had. I felt that if someone copied it, I would become useless, worthless, and replaceable.

Recently I watched someone publicly share their business-building strategy. I know this person, had spoken with them, and had shared this very strategy with them. They liked it so much they asked if they could use it. I said sure. It did feel weird, later, to watch my idea being passed out with no credit of it originating from me.

I could stay attached to the things I innovate and share, and to receiving credit for them, but the reality is that this uncredited sharing will happen again. Knowing this, that attachment wouldn't be healthy.

I can choose instead to see it as me succeeding at my bigger mission: that of propagating new thinking and connection.

Here was evidence of my "thought leadership": my idea was spreading and it wasn't even me doing the work of sharing it, but someone else.

If others in the audience adapted the idea, it would increase that propagation. This is in service of the greater good.

Maybe me abandoning wanting credit for every idea of mine is part of this propagation as well.

I also have new insight on what it is that I do and why I'll never fear feeling like an imposter again:

*My value isn't in the ideas I have. I'm no longer in fear that if those ideas are copied I become worthless. My value is in my ability to **create** the ideas and innovate. There are plenty more where they came from.*

And THAT can never be copied.

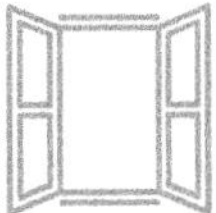

Imagine at this second you know what your real value is that cannot be copied. What is it?

CHAPTER NINETEEN

MY SECRET IDENTITY IS REVEALED

I was recently watching the movie Kill Bill on Netflix. I saw it when it was new and enjoyed revisiting it, especially when there was a scene that jumped out at me with new gravitas. It was a scene between Bill (played by David Carradine) and The Bride (played by Uma Thurman).

This is an excerpt from the movie script of the monologue from that scene.

Bill:

Now, a staple of the superhero mythology is, there's the superhero and there's the alter ego. Batman is actually Bruce Wayne, Spider-Man is actually Peter Parker. When that character wakes up in the morning, he's Peter Parker. He has to put on a costume to become Spider-Man. And it is in that characteristic Superman stands alone. Superman didn't become Superman. Superman was born Superman.

When Superman wakes up in the morning, he's Superman. His alter ego is Clark Kent. His outfit with the big red "S", that's the blanket he was wrapped in as a baby when the Kents found him. Those are his clothes. What Kent wears— the glasses, the business suit—that's the costume. That's the costume Superman wears to blend in with us. Clark Kent is how Superman views us. And what are the characteristics of Clark Kent? He's weak, he's unsure of himself, he's a coward. Clark Kent is Superman's critique on the whole human race.

I started to ponder that quote through my lens as someone recovered from imposter syndrome. What if Superman forgot he was Superman, and adopted Clark Kent as his full-time identity?

He would still be Superman, because that's who he *is*. He just wouldn't recognize it.

When I thought I was a faker, the biggest crime was I was living as a fake to myself. I was not acknowledging the amazing things I had done, that could only have been done by me. I saw them as luck or good timing.

I embodied those Clark Kent traits of weakness and being unsure of myself. I was a coward, and I suffered because of it.

Then I remembered who I am. *I am Superman.* I threw away the Clark Kent costume, because I don't need it anymore. I refuse to wear it.

That's the person you are experiencing now. My greatest pleasure is when I create experiences where I create awe in people, for being nothing more than myself.

And here's a truth I have learned: I am not special. We are all Superman. All of us are walking around in Clark Kent clothing, thinking that's who we're supposed to be.

What if you didn't need to do that? What if that was actually the worst thing you could be doing?

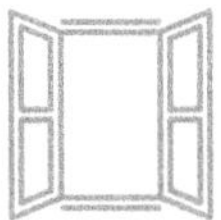

Imagine what changes for you when you realize you are walking around in your own Clark Kent clothing?

What can you do to show your true, most powerful self to the world?

Who benefits from that?

CHAPTER TWENTY

FAILING MY WAY TO MY DREAM LIFE

In the past, I never spoke my failures. I hid them from the world. I projected my strengths and hid my weaknesses. I only spoke about my victories. Yes, that sort of works, and it will impress some types of people, but at some point it just wasn't working for me anymore.

It fed my imposter syndrome. I carried my failures like Marley's chains in *A Christmas Carol*. The chains were my secret shames.

Until one day it changed. As I began to feel more and more gratitude for the life I have today, those failures became a necessary part of creating the life I'm living. If my truth is that I'd never trade the life I'm living at this moment for anything, then I must accept and be grateful for those failures as well.

If they were necessary, then why should I see them as negative?

What if they weren't just neutral, but actual strengths?

What if those same failures, not only helped create the life I have today, they also make me extremely attractive to the rest of the world?

Here are some of my biggest fails:

- I never completed high school. I dropped out. I'd be unemployable if I tried to get a standard job.

- I slept on the floor of my office for two years, homeless, while lying to everyone about it.

- I got myself banned from entering the United States, for working as a DJ without a work visa. That denied me many financial opportunities and essentially ended my career.

- I didn't file my taxes for seven years and had the tax man literally banging at my door.

- Those tax problems made me go through a personal bankruptcy, and I had to start over.

- After my DJ career ended, I had nothing to fall back on. I was so broke I could hardly feed my family. That period lasted for years.

- I've bombed on stage. I've done shows where no one showed up, or I had to endure the humiliation of it not going well.

- I have a massive list of dead projects that went nowhere.

- I hid from my business partner for years, afraid to be on the phone with him. That eventually led me into a crisis I could not avoid any longer.

- Most recently, I abdicated instead of delegated, resulting in a painful two years of transition and rebuilding that personally cost me over a million dollars.

And… the above list has created a life I would not trade away for anything or any amount of money.

I didn't come to this realization overnight. Some of these took many years to become grateful for. Adversity is never enjoyable while you are in the middle of it, and it's even worse when it is by your own hands.

The above list are things done *by* me, not *to* me. That is a key difference. As I learn to forgive myself and be grateful, it is for the things I had and have control over.

All those things have made me who I am today. All of those failures have stories attached to them, about how I grew because of it, or what new opportunities were created because of them. A lot of those failures resulted in me being forged in fire and stronger because of it. They're as necessary to the life I have today as my greatest successes.

I failed my way to my dream life, the life I've created today.

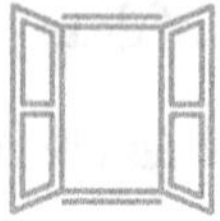

What was your greatest fail and how did it actually facilitate the life you have today?

CHAPTER TWENTY-ONE

I ABDICATED INSTEAD OF DELEGATED AND LEARNED TO FORGIVE MYSELF

At the depths of my crisis—my acute imposter syndrome, my overwhelming anxiety—it got to the point where I felt you could hold a gun to my head and order me to do the work I needed to do, and it still wouldn't get done. You would have to kill me and I would accept my death.

The fact that I was making millions of dollars during this same time period compounded everything to me. I couldn't escape the feeling that I had gotten lucky. That it could all go poof in a moment's notice. That I'd never have this success again.

If there was a time to delegate, it was years earlier. That horse had left the barn and was off in some meadow, hundreds of miles away.

I had wanted out of the business for at least six years before this date. I'd had six years of being extremely unhappy, paralyzed in fear. Fear kept me miserable by not taking action.

And when I finally did take action, I was only capable of a single choice: abdication. I'd take a walk, hand 100% control of everything to my partner, and hope for the best.

How I exited added to my guilt and me beating myself up.

I can forgive myself now. Abdication was the best choice available to me at the time. The best thing I could do was step away. It was going to be messy and had huge risk. Despite that, it was still the best choice left.

It took over two years for that decision to finally conclude. It was painful. The business needed to make a massive reinvestment in itself to make up for me leaving. A new team had to be assembled. They had to start from scratch.

To be on the safe side, I initially tripled the forecasted budget of the new team. Even my conservative budget was wrong, as it ended up taking eight times the money the initial budget projected.

While that new team replaced me, and my partner learned to operate the business without me, I did the work on myself I desperately needed.

Some truths came out:

1. If a gun to my head wasn't going to motivate me to do the work, I can start to forgive myself that it wasn't getting done.

2. I'd never trade this time in my life, these years in my mid-forties to deal with my mental health, for any amount of money.

3. What I accomplished, with no formal education or training, and working solo, was so amazing a team of professionals needed years and millions of dollars to recreate my work.

4. It's always easier to copy something than create it, so not only did I make something incredible, I created it from scratch without following someone else's work.

5. Even though the budget was blown by a factor of 8, it was self-funded. It was funded from the profits of the company I co-founded and software I created. It paid for its own replacement. To this date we've never had an investor and my partner and I own the company 50/50. That is an incredible accomplishment that I'm still absorbing.

6. I'm an artist that creates my version of art. I work alone. I can forgive myself that I didn't transition into management and being a boss.

7. It was painful *and* it all worked out. It was like I was lost in the desert, picked a direction, and started

walking. I can't get upset at myself that there *might* have been a city one mile behind me in the other direction. That was completely unknown to me. I picked a direction and started to go, and I finally emerged from the desert. I lived. I can celebrate that, rather than beat myself up by looking at a map and second-guessing my path.

8. I learned to forgive myself for everything, unconditionally. I don't need to apply logic or make the case. I'm worthy of forgiveness.

9. I was a great partner to my business partner. I was motivated by what would serve him best. There's no point going over the "shoulda/woulda/couldas". In the end it all worked out and I took an incredible risk out of loyalty to him.

10. Sitting here in front of you, writing this, I wouldn't trade anything for this moment. And that includes the pain I endured through my painful abdication. In the end, it has put me right here.

I realize while writing this, self-forgiveness is a theme of mine. It was so necessary for me. Of forgiving myself for mistakes and failures, whether real or imagined. All of those experiences made me who I am today, and for that I am grateful.

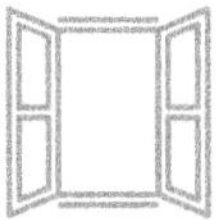

Where in your life can you find self-forgiveness and gratitude for your own story?

Who are you becoming as you embrace that?

CHAPTER TWENTY-TWO

I CAUGHT MYSELF FEELING LIKE A FAKE AGAIN

Despite my best efforts, I still fall into comparing myself with others and then feeling less-than.

It happened this past week. I was doing a bit of research on podcasts I might want to guest on. I did some searches around the idea of life after you leave your business. I found some, and then I started seeing the little bios of the successful "exits" of the guests.

But I've never "exited". Every business I've ever created I ran until it was complete, and then I abandoned it and did something else.

And even now with my webinar company, I abdicated. I abandoned it again. This time was a little different, because my partner took over and runs it without me.

He'd love it if I had a role with the company, but I choose to have zero. I would have sold my share if I could, but I didn't get the deal I wanted. I took the deal I had.

So I don't have a typical exit story that I can trot out for a podcast interview and toot my horn about what the deal was.

And then I realized—shit, I'm feeling it again… this is imposter syndrome. I'm feeling less-than when comparing myself.

At least this time I caught it.

I make my own path, but I was comparing myself with these "traditional" stories once again.

And the ridiculous thing is that I'm fully aware that I'm living a very fulfilled life, one where I score most of my life metrics very high. This is the life I created.

I don't have that sexy "exit" story, and yet I feel alone with my embarrassment of riches. I've achieved and acquired everything I've ever wanted. "More" is no longer the answer to "What do you want?" for me. I have an enviable life of freedom and peace. I spend my days doing whatever I want.

I didn't suffer financially under Covid-19. In fact, things continued to work out for me. My passive income grew multiple times since Covid-19 started. And not in a "my crypto went to the moon—oops, it's back down again" way, but in actual cash I receive every month.

What an achievement, and yet I caught myself thinking I'm unworthy of being a guest on these shows.

The thing is, I've come to learn the power of my story. Doing it differently than everyone else is what makes me so unique and valuable. I'm not a Silicon Valley guy. And even where I am now, I'm doing it in my own unique way.

I actually can't teach anyone how to be successful playing the normal game. I've never done that. And I'm living proof that there are other ways to play and other ways to succeed. There are even other ways to exit.

I teach just by existing.

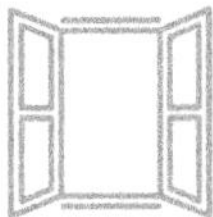

Imagine the next time you find yourself feeling less-than when comparing yourself to others, what did you do to catch it happening? How did you allow yourself some grace instead?

CHAPTER TWENTY-THREE

YOU'RE WATCHING ME MAKE THIS UP

"You're watching me make this up." I can say this to a stranger now, because there is nothing fake about me.

It's been liberating.

I'm not faking 'til I make it. Not anymore. That was a strategy I used effectively for years but not now. I'm showing up as the whole Chris. That is who they are here for. There is no faking that. They're either going to want more of that, or not want it. If they don't want it, that is totally okay and doesn't make me feel any less. As they say, the world would be an extremely boring place if we all wanted the same things.

I'm excited to work with those that want to work with me. That's where the magic will happen.

I want to work with people and missions that excite me. Otherwise, why bother?

For years I would work in solitude, until I had the "gold master" of my project. (A gold master is the finished version of software or a recording, which is used to create duplicates for sale.) I would only share my finalized version with the world when it was beyond criticism and could not be changed.

That worked well. I had a lot of success with that method. My intuition could be trusted. An artist will work on their piece of art until they are done and then display it at a gallery. They don't come back to work on it there. That is how most art is created. That was how I worked.

But I'm ready for a new challenge and have been preparing for it.

I can enter situations and be ready for anything, on one condition: I promise nothing other than to show up as me. Nothing more, nothing less.

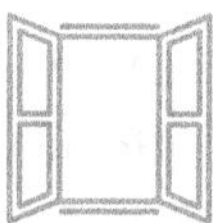

Imagine feeling this liberation in your own life. How does that affect how you show up in the world?

CHAPTER TWENTY-FOUR

STARTING OVER, BUT NOT REALLY

My story involves multiple resets. I've left things I have been successful at and started from scratch over and over.

While that seems true, I also realize it's not really accurate. Each time is a little easier, because with everything I've done, I always start with all the skills and experiences I have accrued up to that point.

I like to visualize myself with a tool belt. I keep adding new tools to it. I've learned to see myself not as the thing I'm doing, but as a distillation of everything I've learned over my life, everything I've done, and everything that makes me *me*. As I start over at a new objective, that "me" is still as strong as it was, and it continues to get stronger all the time.

It's like if you were playing a video game and got to "level up" your character over the span of the game. Then you transfer that character to a new game, but all their levels remain intact.

It's gotten to the point where I'm not even sure what to call myself these days. How do I wrap up all of my life's experiences and knowledge into a neat label?

The answer is, I've stopped trying. I don't label myself any longer, and I've stopped labeling what I do with my days.

I made a list of "what I do now" and filled a page of text with what I do with my days. It's beyond trying to fit into a tidy package.

For a long time when I started something new, I saw myself starting at zero. That is absolutely a false statement. You only start at zero once… at birth.

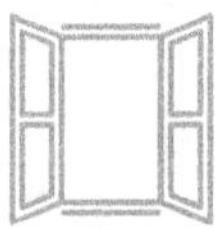

What are the tools on your toolbelt that you've acquired over your entire life and will take with you, no matter what the next "game" you are playing will be?

CHAPTER TWENTY-FIVE

LIFE EXPERIENCE IS NO JOKE

I remember years ago coming across some "diploma mill" that would give you a degree for little effort (and a lot of money). One of the things they'd give you a lot of credit for was "life experience".

At the time I thought that was the biggest joke in the world. Now, in that specific case, it was a joke, because they were just using it as a way to sell you a piece of a paper. But now as I reflect on my life I see the value of life experience.

There is no way that you or I or anyone else don't grow and pick up experiences and skills as we live our lives. (Well, unless you were in a coma for decades.)

For a long time I felt like a faker, faking my way through everything. Now I see myself as a person that has lived a life and built a huge chest of tools from all those years. Some of these are the tools that I'm now sharing with you.

We're all learning, all the time. The tools we collect will be unique to our own journeys, and as you continue on your path, you're going to have every tool you've collected.

Give yourself credit, and dig deep into yourself to figure out what tools you've collected that will benefit your life today. I'm sure you have a ton of transferable skills that will be beneficial in ways you didn't anticipate.

And the ones that you're missing?

You will always be missing tools. As will I. No one will ever know everything about everything.

The difference for me today is I leverage the tools I have, and make it known what I don't have. I'm never going to pretend I have diplomas, for example. If that is what they are looking for, then I'm not the right person for them. I'm the right person for the people who value me and the tools I do bring.

And sometimes I will fail or something doesn't come as fast as I wanted, because I was missing a tool. That's all part of my journey.

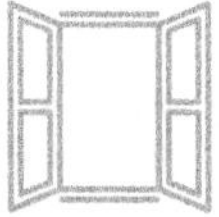

Consider for a moment the path of life you have taken and imagine you have the awareness of all the acquired tools around your toolbelt. What is the most valuable unique tool you've acquired that no one else has?

CHAPTER TWENTY-SIX

YOUR WEAKNESSES ARE YOUR STRENGTHS

This is such a counter-intuitive lesson. I realized the things we see as our weaknesses are actually our strengths and I'm going to demonstrate for you a tool I use.

First, I'm going to create a list. I'm going to try and get into the mindset of what my biggest critics would say about me on this topic:

Top 10 Reasons I'm Not Qualified to Write This Book

1. I'm not a known voice in the guru/self-help world.

2. I've never written a self-help book before. I don't know how they're supposed to be written or what goes into them.

3. While some of the content in this book was drawn from my previous blog posts, I gave myself a 60-day window to create and complete it, though books normally take years to complete.

4. I've made huge life-altering mistakes. Colossal ones that will haunt me for the rest of my life, like getting myself banned from entering the US and a bankruptcy from 2005 that is still a scar on my credit.

5. I'm a high school dropout with no traditional education. I don't have an academic background, nor do I speak as an academic.

6. I don't like to "work". My work on this book is usually contained to an hour or two each morning.

7. Three years ago I was a hot mess living inside a mental prison of my own doing. I'm not your typical expert who can claim a perfect road of success.

8. No one has taught me to do what I'm doing at the moment. All I am is an expert on being me.

9. I don't use social media and don't have a huge number of followers.

10. I'm not special. I'm the same as anyone else.

Despite the above, I'm writing this book anyways.

So that's the list I created about why I'm not qualified. But what if I took that *exact same list* and gave it this title instead:

10 Reasons Why Chris Frolic is a Much-Needed Breath of Fresh Air and What He Has to Say Can Change Your Life

1. I'm not a known voice in the guru/self-help world.

2. I've never written a self-help book before. I don't know how they're supposed to be written or what goes into them.

3. While some of the content in this book was drawn from my previous blog posts, I gave myself a 60-day window to create and complete it, though books normally take years to complete.

4. I've made huge life-altering mistakes. Colossal ones that will haunt me for the rest of my life, like getting myself banned from entering the US and a bankruptcy from 2005 that is still a scar on my credit.

5. I'm a high school dropout with no traditional education. I don't have an academic background, nor do I speak as an academic.

6. I don't like to "work". My work on this book is usually contained to an hour or two each morning.

7. Three years ago I was a hot mess living inside a mental prison of my own doing. I'm not your typical expert who can claim a perfect road of success.

8. No one has taught me to do what I'm doing at the moment. All I am is an expert on being me.

9. I don't use social media and don't have a huge number of followers.

10. I'm not special. I'm the same as anyone else.

Same list. And now, I'm damn proud of it.

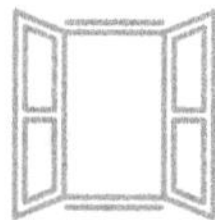

Imagine the power of how you would change from doing this exercise yourself.

What's the list you can create about your greatest weaknesses today, and what's the new title you can give that exact same list?

CHAPTER TWENTY-SEVEN

YOU ARE THE SUM TOTAL OF YOUR ENTIRE LIFE

As someone who has re-invented themselves multiple times in my life, I've grown very comfortable with closing the book on one thing and then moving onto the next. I'm always pondering, "What's next?"

This has been very powerful and has made me nimble and fluid, able to overcome challenges by being open to simply moving on, rather than trying to fix something for too long.

However, I didn't realize there was an unintended side effect to thinking this way. I felt my past was my past, but when I saw it that way, I didn't value it in my present. I failed to fully use everything from my past, because I saw it as something behind me and ancient history.

I was a DJ and rave promoter for ten years. When I retired from that I became a comedy stage hypnotist. Besides some of the basics of being an entrepreneur, I essentially started over. My Chris Frolic hypnotist persona was a new creation.

I had a lot of success in it, but I acted as if I had never done anything else. I didn't speak of my past, and my history was not in my promo materials. In fact, I worried if someone Googled me they'd see my DJ past and that wouldn't help me as a hypnotist. I thought it would reveal I was sort of new at the whole thing, instead of hypnosis being something I'd done for decades.

When I moved on from hypnosis, I did the same thing with my software business. I saw no value in my story as a DJ, promoter, or hypnotist. I didn't even see value in how I sought out my first job as a preteen. I never spoke of any of those things. It was only after I hit my crisis and started looking inward that I started to see how unique I was.

In 2019 I completed my long-gestating memoir, *Requiem for My Rave*. I started work on it fourteen years earlier. I finished the first draft in 2009 and then put it away for a decade, until suddenly it became important to me to finish.

There was something magical about finishing that book then. I revisited that whole part of my life. I got to tell my story. It was a story I had been running away from telling, and it felt good to write it out.

I now know I will always be the rave DJ. It's a part of who I am. I may never spin a record again, but when I get on a stage, any stage, "Anabolic Frolic" shows up, as does "Chris Frolic, comedy stage hypnotist". Not that I'll be hypnotizing people, but I'm that person that is comfortable on the microphone and on stage. I've rocked crowds of tens of thousands of people and I belong on the stage.

And then I took this thinking even further: *I am unique. I am the sum total of my 46 years on this planet. There is literally only one of me in the entire universe. And that makes me priceless and awesome.*

I stand before you re-integrated and complete. Unique and priceless. What ways can you sense that?

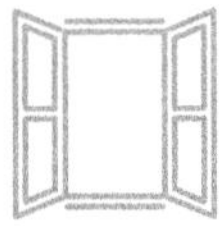

What from your past have you closed off like a book, and how might you re-integrate it into who you are today?

PART FOUR
PEACE
ACHIEVED

CHAPTER TWENTY-EIGHT

I STILL GET SCARED I CAN'T DO IT AGAIN

At the worst of the depths of my imposter syndrome, I felt like Bernie Madoff. I had fooled the world, or at least that is what I thought.

A few years ago, as I looked for ways to spend my time, I didn't even feel qualified to judge a high-school business competition. Seeing those teenagers in their suits and ties, future MBA students, was too intimidating; here I was, the high school dropout who didn't even own a suit. It didn't matter that I had this huge history of things I've done. I kept telling myself I had gone about it so differently, I had nothing to offer anyone.

If you've read this book from the start, you know what changed for me: it was when I realized that these exact things I was ashamed of, my unconventional path, my non-traditional education, the fact that I don't seek permission, my self-reliance, the audaciousness of my story—those exact things make me great. That I had accomplished everything I did the way I did it was why I should be proud of myself. I was the opposite of an imposter. I was the real deal. I finally started to see it for myself.

Here's the thing though—I'm still scared.

Yes, I did all those things, and yes they were amazing and awesome, and yet *I'm still scared I can't do it again.*

I'm older now. Back in the day I was a young kid with nothing to lose. Now I have a lot to lose.

Back in the day I could do what it takes. I could sleep on the floor to make it happen.

I'm not willing to do that anymore. I have responsibilities and a family to support. It's not just about me.

I have a life I've created that I love. I'm not willing to trade it away.

A lot of how I made things possible in the past involved playing on the edge, sometimes for years. I burned my ships, making it impossible to go back. It was survive or die.

That's actually the only way I know how to do things. I've never created something from this place that I'm in today, one of abundance. Complacency is my biggest enemy now.

There's still something in me that wants to make an impact. I feel very much like I have unfinished business. What's new for me is to make it work from this current place that I'm in.

Because I don't know how to do this, it's scary. I wonder if I still *can* do it.

I feel like an older boxer lacing up their boots, wondering if they still have it in them.

And yet—no matter how scary the not-knowing is—I'm going to have to find a new way to do it.

My hope is someday I can look back at this time and say to myself, "See, you did do it. The fear didn't stop you. There was nothing to be scared of." But I don't have a crystal ball, so that means I'll be dealing with the fear until then.

But the fear is also valuable. It tells me that I have a fire left in me. I'm not done yet. If I was as "retired" as I say I am, I wouldn't care.

I use fear as a compass, as you'll be discovering in the next chapter.

Today, it was about *admitting* I'm scared.

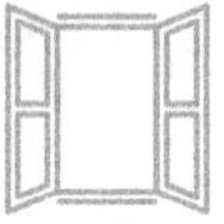

Imagine three years from now, looking back at a time when you found a way to forgive yourself after reading this book. What was the first thing you did to help forgive yourself that then allowed some grace that fear will always be present in your life?

CHAPTER TWENTY-NINE

THE MOST POWERFUL TOOL I HAVE

f I had to share only one thing, it would be these three words:

"What scares me?"

That prompt is responsible for so many of the big stories in my life. I did the scary thing, and something incredible happened.

And here's the actual truth of it: once done, that thing ended up being no big deal.

It's amazing how big a mountain we can create of these choices in our lives. The explanation is that our brains haven't kept up with our human society—our brains are primed for primitive survival and constant fight-or-flight. But many of us now live lives of unimaginable comfort and security, compared to all of human existence. For many of us, because our lives are not actually in constant danger anymore, our brains will attach that fear to other things instead.

Acts as simple as speaking up, sharing an opinion, or making an offer can easily trigger that deep fear.

And here's the extra burn: that risk that our brain is trying to protect us from, usually involves a fear of changing the status quo… which is often the exact thing we should be doing.

I felt afraid recently when giving feedback to someone on a forum. I wrestled with whether I should. I wrestled with the idea of how what I had to say would be received by them. I was scared of upsetting them. I was scared that I might be over-stepping and they would not like me.

I went back and forth, and then ultimately decided to take my own medicine. I did what scared me and said what I wanted to say. I realized I would be denying them my voice if I gave in to the fear. That would be a terrible thing to do.

And those kinds of experiences are part of why I created this book and shared it with you. What value would I have denied you today had I given into the fear?

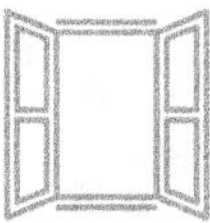

So...

What scares you?

CHAPTER THIRTY

I'M PROUD OF MYSELF

There's a feeling I've been regularly experiencing lately. The best word I can use to describe it is "pride".

Pride sometimes is seen as negative, especially when it's about comparing yourself with others. Pride can be used to compensate for one's shortcomings, and then create a story of why they're better than someone else.

On a recent Zoom call, during a discussion of pride, a colleague from Germany shared her experience with the history of her country and what can happen with nationalistic pride.

I acknowledge those examples, but I'm left with "pride" still being the closest word I have to describe this feeling I get regularly.

It's a pride in myself. A self-validation. When I take action that's in line with my core self, I'm proud of myself. It has nothing to do with comparing myself to anyone.

Now, as I write this today, looking back I see what I did as the amazing achievements that they truly were. I broke every rule that existed.

I became a best-selling DJ because I dared to be one. It's the act of daring and the action I took that makes me feel proud.

I wrote a memoir that took me fourteen years to complete. It's the act of completing it, of re-integrating that part of my life back into who I am today, of telling my story, that I'm proud of.

I'm proud of re-inventing myself multiple times over in my life, in wild ways, like being a stage hypnotist.

I'm proud of creating StealthSeminar in my own unique way.

I engineered solutions to every problem I faced, in the most creative ways you could imagine.

When I decided to step away, it required a huge team of coders and millions of dollars to replace the work I had created by myself.

I didn't follow any rule from the tech startup playbook, because that book didn't exist to me.

I didn't follow any rule from the business management playbook, because that book didn't exist to me.

I didn't follow any rule from any book. I went my own way.

And now that company has existed for over 10 years. We achieved what almost everyone fails at.

Today I understand that my ability to *not* follow a playbook is what makes me *me*. I own the shit out of that. I'm proud of it. It gives me pleasure when I do it.

"Greg Fisher" has been retired. "Chris Frolic" stands before you as a complete and authentic person.

I can't go back in time and do anything different. As painful as the process was, I wouldn't be the person I am today without the pain of that part of my life.

All I can do today is share my story, and maybe help someone out there by them knowing that they aren't alone, that I've been through it, and I got through it.

This was a feeling that was missing for many years when I was a tortured imposter and had zero pride for the work I did, no matter how much money I was making.

Something has changed in me, and that makes me feel good about myself. That sense of pride feeds me.

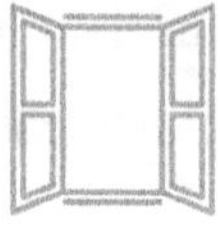

Just suppose you already knew the smallest step you could take to allow yourself to feel proud of your actions. What is it?

CHAPTER THIRTY-ONE

I'M RUNNING MY OWN RACE

Every time I get caught in a thinking trap about what I "should" be doing or am "supposed" to be doing, it's because I've fallen into comparing myself with other people.

I've never sold a company. I don't know how to "exit". Everything I've ever done in the past I ran until I was complete and I moved on and did something else. I abdicated instead of delegated and reduced my role with my webinar business to zero. I receive monthly dividends, for as long as my partner wants to run the company or sell it. I don't have some sexy story to peddle for the masses about my big sale.

I don't know how to attract investors. I don't know how to be funded. I don't know how to be an investor in anything other than myself. I don't know how to run a money-losing business for years.

All I know is how to create businesses with no investors and create profit from day one, because I had to to survive.

There's no point comparing myself with the headline stories on the websites I read.

And yet… I'm living my dream life. A life filled with gratitude. Every day I get up to do the things I find important and give me joy. I work on myself primarily. I show up powerfully in the communities I'm a part of, and I give the best I've got to give with everyone I encounter.

So what does it matter if I'm not written up on some large website?

On all my major life metrics, I score myself highly. Who am I comparing myself against and why would I want to let my impression of them reduce my own life satisfaction?

I put immense value on the freedom with my days; I often have zero things scheduled. I try and limit my Zooms to a single meeting per day, at the most. In a world that preaches "crushing it" and worships overworking, that type of schedule just isn't spoken about. I create more like an artist, when it strikes me. I'm writing this at 4 PM on a Sunday, because that was when I was inspired to write it, not when I scheduled it.

My solution is reminding myself that *I'm running my own race*. I need to stop comparing myself with anyone else. If I'm hitting my personal benchmarks, it ends with that.

Someone is always going to have "more" than me. My personal race doesn't involve chasing that.

Someone is going to get more attention than me. Well, I like being a "sage on the mountain". That's the race I'm running. I have a private email list and that's it. I don't chase followers, Likes, or subscribers.

If that's the race I'm running, then I need to remember that *that's* the race I'm running! I can't be in two races at once.

And the beautiful thing about running my own race? I always win.

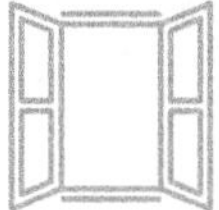

Whose race are you running?

What can you do to start running your own race instead?

CHAPTER THIRTY-TWO

MY GREATEST ACCOMPLISHMENT

This past year I was asked what my greatest accomplishment of the past decade would be. As I thought about it, I realized the thing I was most proud was not about any financial achievement, or goal achieved. It was about coming to a place of deep understanding of myself, and then from that place being able to write a document articulating that, both for myself and to share with others.

While I was working on it, I reconnected with some colleagues on Zoom, and mentioned in passing that I was working on it.

They asked, "Can we hear it?"

I froze. It wasn't ready. It was still a work in progress. But I decided to read it anyway.

Something transformed in me by the end of my reading (perhaps better described as a performance). I realized I had shared a list of truths about myself. I didn't even need to hear their feedback, because it was already all true for me. I felt good.

The listeners were moved. They felt the power of what I had just done, and they all shared how it affected them. It was as if I had performed a powerful piece of music or poetry that transcended.

I also realized in that moment that it didn't matter if I didn't think it was complete. The truth is that it will evolve and change over my entire life as I get new clarity and insights about myself. It will always be incomplete, until the day that I die. Then it will be complete.

I often think it could be read at a memorial service of mine. It's a way to share with the mourners not what I did, but who I was.

And I was a changed person the next day. Something had changed in me, permanently. I had a confidence in myself I didn't have before. I felt comfortable in my own skin.

I came up with the title "My Statement of Being" for that document, because that is literally what it is.

I will never feel like a fake again because I refuse to feel that way. The Statement of Being allows me to reconnect with myself whenever I need to.

It also allows me to share who I am with others. I often read it to someone before I explore working with them, because I want them to know who I am and what they are getting, and for me not to pretend to be anything else.

I am always exploring new experiences and opportunities, but I am never again feeling like an imposter, because I completely disclose who I am first.

Only from that place will I agree to take on that new challenge. No more faking it 'til I make it. I show up now and just *be* it. Be me. And that feels good.

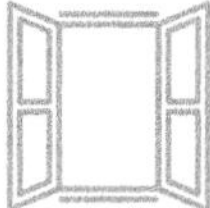

Why would it be important to you to feel this way in your own life?

CHAPTER THIRTY-THREE

CHRIS' STATEMENT OF BEING

1. I go by my chosen name, Chris Frolic. It's a name that means something to me.

2. I am audacious. I eat the words "it can't be done" for breakfast.

3. I take pride in my role with Robin and my children. It is a privilege to serve my family powerfully. My family gives me great fulfilment.

4. I create the life I want to live and live it.

5. I feel gratitude every day.

6. I share my wisdom with all who want it.

7. I am unique and priceless. I am the sum total of all my experiences, things I've learned, and my mistakes.

8. I love myself unconditionally, and I embrace and love my unconventional ways.

9. I forgive myself unconditionally.

10. I get pleasure from zagging when everyone else is zigging.

11. I am enough, yet I will never stop striving to be more.

12. People are impacted from being around me and I honor that responsibility.

13. I am a great communicator. I'm a natural spontaneous storyteller and I collect stories to tell. I can take abstract or complicated ideas and make them accessible. I speak with metaphors.

14. I understand it's not about doing more, but being more.

15. I like playing a big game. I create games where I win the moment I decide to play them.

16. I know that my fear of regret is greater than the fear of the thing, and that motivates me to do things *because* they are scary.

17. When I'm having fun, magic happens.

18. Money is a byproduct of my awesomeness. I love shining and showing my awesomeness.

19. I live my life as a permanent vacation. My schedule is fluid and open. I can do whatever I want, whenever I want. I enjoy taking naps in the afternoon and having days that don't have a single thing scheduled.

20. I embrace not knowing. It's where new things are discovered or created.

21. I am a trailblazer. I know what it's like to create something from nothing. I love the joy of doing something for the first time. I enjoy doing things *because* they've never been done before.

22. I know that the world is best served by the strongest version of me.

23. They say, "You can't take someone deeper than you've gone yourself." Well, I've gone pretty damn deep. I've been immersed in this process for years. This is my work.

24. I seek to create feelings in myself, and I can create them in others.

25. I know how to create experiences. I can execute a fully realized version from a thought in my mind.

26. I take action on my thoughts decisively and without hesitation.

27. I feel pride from self-validation. Being true to myself drives me to take action and anything past that is a cherry on top.

28. I conduct energy.

29. I fight for humanity.

30. I am a changing state of matter in the universe and I know my consciousness is temporary and will cease one day.

To watch Chris read his Statement of Being, visit this link:
WWW.CHRISFROLIC.COM/BONUS/

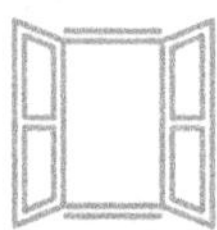

How much of my Statement of Being do you feel you experienced while reading this book?

How connected do you feel to me?

What from my Statement of Being do you share in your own life?

Imagine a future, 3 years from now, of how your life has changed from creating this type of connection between yourself and others.

How has that impacted your life?

CHAPTER THIRTY-FOUR

HOW TO CREATE A STATEMENT OF BEING

A Statement of Being is a statement of who you are and who you've been. It's not about the person you want to be, your aspirations, your hopes and dreams. It's a statement of your truth.

I realized my statements were true when I retroactively tested them. I imagined myself at an earlier age, and then asked myself if it was true then. Almost all of them were true when I was twenty years old. Some were true when I was a child.

Not all of them were true for all of my life, as some of them became true at different points of my life, or were affected by my life changing.

No labels are used. The statement of the pride I feel in service to my family discusses how I feel; I did not use the label husband or father, because this isn't about roles.

Labels are temporary. These statements are permanent.

None of these statements are given to me externally; they came from within me. No one can take them away from me, and I don't need anyone to agree or disagree with them. They just are.

Every statement has a version of "I am".

Each of the statements are of you at your best. This is not a complete mirror exercise. It's about identifying your best strengths, so what were once "happy accidents" you can call upon in a more intentional manner.

And now that I've said all this I must add this statement: *I made this all up.* This was a creation from within me. There are no rules here. These are the rules I came up with for myself and what felt right to me. I would never say these are the official rules for everyone.

Create what feels right for you. I won't come knocking on your door to tell you you did it wrong.

You might even want to title yours something different, something that better describes what you created.

Start out by writing whatever amount feels right. Give yourself permission that it will never be truly done. It will grow and evolve over time. You can revisit any of your statements at any time, refine them, replace them with something that feels better, add to it, and drop others as needed.

I settled on 30, and I've aimed to keep it there, but that was just a number I landed on.

And then read it for others. Perform it as you would a song or poetry. Share yourself with the world and feel that change that happens from within as you do.

The process of creating a Statement of Being isn't completed until you are witnessed speaking it.

In the future, keep your Statement of Being handy, so you can reference it and remember to stay aligned with it. That will be when you are at your most powerful.

I'm excited for you.

What was the biggest piece of value you have taken from this book?

CHAPTER THIRTY-FIVE

THIS IS ME

And that's what I've got for you. I think about how I wrote "Don't hold back" twice in my notes when I started on this book. That I wrote it twice made me take notice. I accepted the challenge and you hold the result in your hands.

I've done great things, and I've had great failures. I enjoy leaning into that narrative more and more because I know it's not one that is told regularly.

I'm not an entrepreneur. I'm not a DJ. I'm not a coach. I'm not an author. I'm more than a father and husband. I'm not a label.

I *cannot* be labeled. I *refuse* to be labeled.

I'm Chris Frolic.

And that's why I'll never feel like a fake again.

Take a moment to imagine you and I had a meeting to debrief about your experience with this book.

What advice do I have for you that is the most important thing you need to hear right now?

If you're like me, these words are always present in your life, and you might be asking them now.

I'm curious to hear from you. What is next for you?

You can use this link to tell me:
WWW.CHRISFROLIC.COM/CONTACT/

I enjoy having freedom in my life and path, so I don't want to permanently record my future intentions here. You can visit this link to find out more about my current activities:
WWW.CHRISFROLIC.COM/NOW/

HOW YOU CAN HELP

'm taking a page from my "Turn your weaknesses into strengths" strategy here. I choose to live a decelerated life outside of social media. That means I don't have a huge following to promote to. I am a "Sage on the Mountain". As of the time I completed this book, I maintained an invitation-only email list with a maximum of 100 people who apply to be on it (the Frolic 100).

That means this book can only reach the people it can most help if you are a part of facilitating that. Who do you know that would have their life changed from reading this book?

Imagine how they might benefit if you were to gift them this best-kept secret?

What if you were to point at the mountain and let someone know what wisdom lies for them atop it?

You can also help by posting a favorable review on Amazon for others to discover.

Thank you.

A C K N O W L E D G E M E N T S
A N D   G R A T I T U D E

’d like to mention the following people for their contributions to this book:

Robin Frolic, you'll always be the love of my life. Thank you for your amazing work editing this book and showing me you want to help me as much as I want to help you.

Geoff Ronning, for being an incredible business partner that helped facilitate this chapter of my life. Geoff was also a beta reader.

Mung-Ling Tsui, for covering me with a blanket and telling me nothing bad was going to happen.

Tim Forrest, for recognizing that I had something powerful to share and being a witness to it. Tim was also a beta reader.

Tom Lancaster, for stepping forward to be a beta reader when I didn't think to ask for help.

David Newman, for your years of friendship and pinball community. David was also a beta reader.

Sandra Harder-Prophet, for the belly laughs. Sandra was also a beta reader.

The Frolic 100, you've assembled for a reason: to be part of what I create. Thank you.

The PK2 Dream Team, you watched me crack open.

Akiko Takagi, for preparing yourself for how to best support me every time you see me dancing on the edge.

Rich Litvin, for letting me play in your sandbox.

The Members of 4PC, for watching me play as big as I dare to and cheering me on while I do it.

ABOUT THE AUTHOR

After this entire book, I don't think there's anything more that needs to be said.